STIRLING

A Stroll Down Memory Lane

Elma Lindsay

Stirling District Libraries
1995

© Stirling District Libraries
1995

Published by
Stirling District Libraries

ISBN 1 870542 30 4

Printed by
Cordfall Ltd, Glasgow
0141-332 4640

INTRODUCTION

Mid 1993, the District Libraries' Local History Officer, seconded part-time to the Smith Art Gallery & Museum, was asked by the Library Service to prepare a series of old photographs, with accompanying text, for publication in the *Stirling Observer*.

In February 1994 the series, culled from the collection of the Smith Art Gallery and Museum, duly appeared in the *Stirling Observer*. The original intention had been a monthly article, but such was the interest shown by readers of the *Observer* that before long the photographs were appearing weekly. The photographs were selected for their content and for their general appeal; consequently there is no particular theme, other than 'the past'. Linking them together for this booklet is merely a geographic progression, from Bridge of Allan to St Ninians, with a detour to the Castle via Baker Street, then down to Dumbarton Road by way of Spittal Street.

There are too many exclusions - John Cowane, Robert Spittal, James Allen, Mar's Wark, Argyll's Ludging, the railway, for example - for this to be anything other than a pictorial reminiscence session. It is what the title says it is, merely 'A Stroll Down Memory Lane'.

Three successive local history officers have worked on this series. The first, Jayne Stephenson, carried out the original research, but left Stirling in August 1993 to take up a post in Tain. She died in a tragic drowning accident in May 1994, and this little booklet is dedicated to her memory.

ACKNOWLEDGEMENTS

One of the most important parts of a Local History Collection is its photographs. The majority of these used in the series came from the Smith Art Gallery and Museum, but we are indebted to the following for lending their own photographs, which have been copied and added to the collection.

Kinross Showroom; P6 Craigs School: Misses C & M Booth. Sterlini Commercial School Outing; Miss M M Macguire. Royal Visit Crowd; Coronation Bowling Match: Mrs M Lamb. Baptist Church and North Church: Whylers Photographs, Stirling. Lawsons, all photographs: Mrs E Macintosh. Auction Mart; Boating Team: the estate of the late Mr A Ross, per Mr G Young. Bannockburn Soup Kitchen; Bannockburn Co-op Van: Mrs M Lamont. 1 Pitt Terrace: Mrs E B Park. Municipal Building Foundation Stone: Mr D F Gardner. REME Marchpast: ABRO, Stirling. Stirling Old Bridge and Stirling New Bridge: Mr A D S MacPherson. Drummond's Fire: Mr W Gavin. Lipton's, Barnton Street: Mrs E Stevenson. Cambuskenneth Bridge; Invitation; Randolph Road: Mrs H Miller.

If you have photographs of local interest which could be copied for either the Library or Museum collection, the Local History Officer would be pleased to hear from you.

In compiling this collection, every attempt has been made to locate the original owner of the photograph, for permission to publish it. In some instances, this has proved to be impossible, and apology is made to anyone who inadvertently has slipped through the net.

The compiler accepts full responsibility for errors of accuracy, and would welcome corrections. If you have further information regarding the content of any of the photographs, that would be most welcome too.

Assistance is acknowledged with gratitude to colleagues in the Smith Art Gallery and Museum, Stirling District Libraries and Central Regional Archives Department. Particular thanks are due to Mrs Irene McKenzie and Mrs Mary McTaggart, Support Services, Library Headquarters, for deciphering and rendering readable the original draft of the text.

Map by courtesy of Stirling Tourist Association. *Grid references appear after captions.*

The start of this nostalgic journey is at . . .

Bridge of Allan, 3$^1/_2$ miles to the north of Stirling, which modestly assumed the title of 'Queen of Scottish Spas' following Sir Robert Abercromby's discovery of mineral wells on his Airthrey Estate in the early 1800s, and his astute promotion of their efficacious properties. The subsequent flow of visitors intent on taking the waters led inevitably to a proliferation of prestigious tourist and residential accommodation, the latter further encouraged by the arrival of the railway in 1848. The station closed in 1965, but was reopened in May 1985, and although the spas are no longer operating, Airthrey Estate is now the source of cerebral effervescence, being the home of the University of Stirling, and Bridge of Allan itself is a bustling, lively town.

Memorial Park,
Bridge of Allan.

The Stirling Tram Car

This open topped tram, photographed at the terminus in Henderson Street, made its appearance in the summer months and was operated by the Stirling and Bridge of Allan Tramway Company. The tram company had started in 1874 and ran a service between Stirling and Bridge of Allan, a journey which took about 25 minutes.

In the early part of this century the company went into decline. Plans to electrify the line had never come to fruition and petrol driven buses were making an appearance and were proving stiff competitors. By 1919 things were in a very sorry state and the local papers were full of complaints about the condition of the vehicles, and especially of the horses. One writer to the *Observer*, signing himself 'Disappointed', complained about the emaciated state of the horses. The next week, signing himself 'Depressed', he complained of a horse dropping dead whilst he was on the tram. Finally, on February 5th 1920 the company folded and so the last remaining horse-drawn tramway in Scotland closed down.

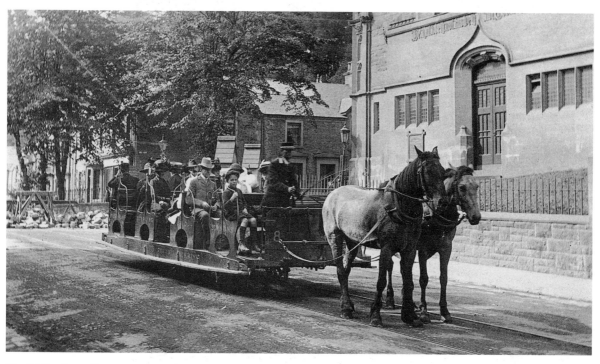

The Stirling Tram Car.

Bridge of Allan War Memorial

The War Memorial in Bridge of Allan was unveiled on Saturday, 26 May 1923 on a site opposite the Museum Hall provided by Mr Edmund Pullar of Westerton House, Bridge of Allan. Mr Pullar himself performed the unveiling ceremony shown here in an appalling downpour of rain. The first wreath was placed on the memorial by Provost Innes on behalf of the Town Council in memory of the 81 local soldiers who had fallen in World War 1.

Bridge of Allan War Memorial.

Wallace Monument

The choice of Stirling as the site of the Wallace Monument was simply to prevent any conflict between Glasgow and Edinburgh, and it was with some relief that members of the National Wallace Monument Movement saw Stirling as a solution to the problem, on neutral ground and overlooking Stirling Bridge, scene of Wallace's great victory of 1297.

The proposal for a monument to honour Scotland's national hero was put forward in the 1830s, raised by a group of prominent Scots who formed a National Wallace Monument Movement at a time when Scotland was experiencing a resurgence of nationalism. Initial enthusiasm petered out however, and not until the 1850s did the movement reappear in the press. The proprietor of the 'Glasgow Daily Bulletin' took up the cause, suggesting the monument should be placed on Glasgow Green, and at this point the Reverend Charles Rogers of Stirling made the tactful suggestion of the Abbey Craig. Approval of Provost, Council and Stirling locals having been sought and given, an energetic campaign was set in motion to raise subscriptions. By 1859 there was enough money to advertise for designs, and entries flooded in from artists and architects alike. The original design accepted depicted the Scottish Lion trampling on a monster, but this was later rejected and after a fresh appeal for designs, those of the existing monument were chosen. The foundation stone was laid on 24 June 1861 by the Duke of Atholl, and a crowd of about 70,000 enjoyed bands, parades and entertainments in King's Park. Relations between Mr Rogers and the committee soured at this point over the disappearance of some funds, so the inauguration ceremony of the Monument on 11th September 1869 was a very low key affair by comparison. It had cost over £10,000 to build, and was handed over to the Town Council with very little celebration. It is now administered by Loch Lomond, Stirling and Trossachs Tourist Board.

Wallace Monument.
(A10)

A Stirling-built Aircraft

This 'canard' or tail-first biplane was designed and constructed in 1909 at the Grampian Engineering and Motor Company at Causewayhead run by brothers Harold, Frank and Archibald Barnwell.

It was driven by a 40 horsepower engine and its first trials took place at a farm in Cornton where it attained a speed of 25 miles per hour, although it never left the ground. Subsequently it reached the necessary speed for take-off and flew 80 yards at a height of 12 feet before it came to grief.

The Barnwell brothers continued their flying experiments and in 1911 Harold won the Law Prize of £50 for the first half-mile flight by an all-Scottish aeroplane.

Harold and Frank soon moved south to follow their careers in the aviation industry. Harold joined Vickers Ltd as their chief test pilot and was killed flying a prototype Vickers FB26 on 25th August 1917. Frank went to the British and Colonial Aeroplane Company where he was responsible for many highly successful designs, including the Bristol Scout, the Bulldog, the Blenheim and the Beaufort. He too was killed flying a small private plane, the Barnwell Weekender, on its second test flight on August 2nd 1938.

A Stirling-built Aircraft. (B9)

Rubber Company of Scotland, Forthvale Works, Stirling

The Rubber Company, established at the turn of the century, was a major employer in Stirling. It made a wide variety of goods from rubber chamber pots to, during the Second World War, submarine floats. One lady, interviewed for the oral history archive in the Smith Museum, remembers her time at the Works with great fondness. "When I started in the 1920s I started making hot water bottles. Then I made rubber gloves for electricians. We made up gloves so they could withstand 20,000 volts. We got one week's holiday with no pay but it was a great place to work. It was taken over by Porters and they stopped making hand made bottles and everything became mechanised."

The factory continued under Porters until the mid 1980s, when it was briefly taken over by the Scandura Company, then by the Gates Rubber Company which eventually closed the works down with the loss of 37 jobs in July 1992.

Rubber Company of Scotland:
Sheeting Team
(Back row l-r) *Albert Coleman,*
James Mason, J Glennie
(Front row l-r) *Alex*
Buchannan, Oly Derrick. (D7)

The Old Bridge, Stirling

The Old Bridge dates from the fifteenth century, and is one of the best examples of a medieval bridge still standing in Scotland. For centuries, it was the only crossing over the Forth into Stirling, a matter of considerable strategic importance not lost on Major-General Blakeney, Hanovarian Governor of Stirling Castle in 1745. On his orders, the arch nearest the town was dismantled in late December to prevent a rendezvous between Prince Charles Edward Stewart's army, recently arrived in Glasgow after the humiliating defeat at Derby, and Jacobite reinforcements from France and Ireland, biding their time in Doune, Dunblane and Bridge of Allan. This put the local people at some inconvenience, and the town council was obliged to provide a ferry service until the bridge was repaired in 1749. For this, passengers were charged 6d Scots.

Stirling Old Bridge. (E7)

At its broadest point, the bridge is only 13 feet wide, which, even in the eighteenth century was insufficient to cope with the volume of traffic, to the extent that the council banned loaded carts from crossing, insisting that loads be removed from the carts and rolled across separately. In 1821, Thomas Telford's opinion was sought by the council on the advisability of widening the bridge. He was strongly opposed to this idea and advised building a new stone one further down the river. One of the leading engineers of the day was Robert Stevenson, grandfather of Robert Louis Stevenson, and he it was who designed the New Bridge, opened in 1833.

At the time this photograph was taken, possibly in the 1950s or early 60s, there was a farm, Laurencecroft, behind the tenements, and a local man, brought up in the area, recalls watching cattle from the farm making their way over the bridge, unsupervised by either farmhand or collie, towards their pasture at Bridgehaugh.

In the background looms Gowan Hill, site of Jacobite troops during the Siege of Stirling Castle in January 1746. On the Heading Hill sits the Beheading Stone, alleged site of early executions, alongside two old cannons brought from the Castle in 1904.

Salmon Fishers on the Forth

The River Forth was an abundant source of salmon in the 15th and 16th centuries. Early Burgh Council Minutes record fishermen being paid to provide salmon for the royal table at the castle. By the 17th century, however, salmon stocks were declining. In 1696 the town council built Fisher Row, a group of 6 houses at the foot of Castle Hill to the East of Raploch, to accommodate fishermen and their families. However the experiment never really worked because of the limited supply of salmon, and by the early 1700s none of the houses were leased to fishermen. Individual boat owners continued to work in teams on the Forth using nets as shown in this photograph taken at the turn of the century.

Nowadays little or no netting takes place on the upper tidal reaches of the Forth and fishing is restricted to the individual angler.

Salmon Fishers on the Forth.

Stirling Harbour

Stirling Harbour at Riverside was a thriving port for both cargo and passengers until the end of last century. After this it went into decline and was used very little after the First World War when all small ports on the Forth were closed to private shipping.

Timber, wood and oil were the main imports to Stirling; cloth was a major export. The Haldane Cooperage at Riverside also exported flat-pack barrels – a forerunner of the DIY kitchen perhaps! Wilson and Sons, Shipowners, of Stirling held a contract with the government for the shipment of stores to army and navy depots and that is one of the reasons that the government decided to establish the Ordnance Stores at Forthside.

During last century, too, pleasure steamers plied their trade from Stirling to Leith and Granton and excursion traffic reached its peak in the 1880s and 1890s. However, competition from motor transport and the physical difficulties of navigating the Forth, mean that a boat tied up at Stirling is a thing of the past.

Stirling Harbour. (F8)

Where there is a river, there are boats, where there are boats there is business – and pleasure. Although Stirling Amateur Boating Society has graced the local sporting scene since 1893, it did not aspire to a boathouse until 1906, and the unusual building is still a familiar sight.

(left) Stirling Amateur Boating Society Club House. (E7)

(middle) The paddle steamer 'Edinburgh Castle' on the Forth near Stirling.

(bottom) The crew that won the Rose Bowl Maiden Championship of Scotland 1921, T McDougal, H Brunton, H Cardno, A Ross (strike), W Scoular, Cox.

Cambuskenneth Ferry

For centuries the ferry to Cambuskenneth was a vital link for the residents of the village, providing a direct route to the town without the need to travel through Causewayhead.

During last century the ferry was at its busiest in July when the berry fair was held in Cambuskenneth. The village was renowned for its market gardens, and gooseberries and strawberries were sold on fair days. Italian ice cream sellers and musicians added a carnival flavour to the day.

In the 1900s the fairs reached their peak and an account in the Stirling Journal talks of 12 and more people being crammed into the small ferry for the penny journey across the Forth.

Cambuskenneth Ferry.
(F9)

Cambuskenneth Bridge

In the 1930s, the council decided to build a footbridge across to Cambuskenneth; this photograph was taken in August 18th 1935 and shows the ferry still operating, but the scaffolding of the new bridge seen in the background, almost complete and waiting for the official opening on Wednesday 23rd October 1935.

The ribbons were cut by Mrs Macintosh, wife of the Provost, and by Mrs Harvey, wife of Captain Harvey, Convener of Stirling County Council. Following short speeches by Captain Harvey and by Provost Macintosh, presentations of silver fruit dishes were made to their wives by representatives of Messrs Christian and Neilsen, the designers and builders, and after a spirited rendering of the National Anthem, the entire party was taken into town for afternoon tea at the Golden Lion Hotel. After the bridge opened, the ferry was no longer required, and the ferryman, Tom Dow, seen here with two lady passengers, retired. It was not a local photographer who recorded the scene here, but John Moodie, from East Wemyss in Fife.

(right) *Cambuskenneth Ferry. (F9)*
(below) *Invitation.*

The Provost, Magistrates, and Councillors of the Royal Burgh
of Stirling, and the County Council of Stirlingshire
request the pleasure of the company of

Mr & Mrs Thomas Dow

at the Opening of the Bridge between Stirling
and Cambuskenneth Abbey,
on Wednesday, 23rd October, 1935, at 3.15 p.m.

R.S.V.P. to Mr. David B. Morris,
Town Clerk, Stirling, not later
than MONDAY, 21st October.

For the convenience of guests, omnibuses will be provided as follows :—
For County Council representatives omnibuses will leave Viewforth at 2.50 p.m.
For Town Council representatives omnibuses will leave the Municipal
Buildings, Corn Exchange Road, at 3 o'clock.

[OVER

Even as early as the 1840s Cambuskenneth was a favourite spot for outings on summer Sundays, and a local businessman, Peter Drummond, one of a well known seed merchant's family, was so appalled at what he regarded as such blatant desecration of the Sabbath, that he took it upon himself to point out to the erring masses the error of their ways. Realising the enormity of this task, he hit on the idea of producing religious tracts, which he distributed to the Sunday sinners. This was the start of the Stirling Tract Enterprise founded in 1848, an extraordinary venture which continued right up to 1980, producing literally thousands of religious tracts which were dispatched all over the world. Drummond eventually made this his full-time business, which was so successful, not only he, but the Post Office, required larger premises.

William Kennedy

Cambuskenneth was a centre of artistic activity between 1880-1920, largely due to the establishment of a teaching studio by Joseph Denovan Adam R.S.A., who lived in Craigmill House from 1887 until his death in 1896. Denovan Adam was recognised as one of the foremost animal painters of his day, and this was the principal subject taught at Craigmill. For teaching purposes he kept a small herd of Highland cattle, together with dogs, sheep, and cattle, which roamed free in the park. An outdoor studio was built in the park, which allowed artists to view the animals in all weathers, and to paint from real life.

(left) Ferry Orchard House. (E9)
(below) William Kennedy.

During the summer months, the studio attracted large numbers of artists, including the famous 'Glasgow Boys', attracted also by the orchards, tree-lined river bank, picturesque ruined abbey, and the old thatched and red-tiled whitewashed cottages. This, together with the opportunity to meet and exchange ideas with other artists made Craigmill an attractive alternative to town studios. Pictured here is Ferry Orchard House, where many of the artists lodged, and 'Glasgow Boy' William Kennedy, painting in the Cambuskenneth orchards, the Abbey Craig in the background.

Bridge Clock Tower

The Bridge Clock Tower at the Union Street roundabout was gifted to the town of Stirling by Provost David Bayne. The inauguration ceremony shown here took place on Saturday 17th September 1910, the Provost himself presiding, and his daughter cutting the ribbon which set the works in motion. After the ceremony, the invited guests retired to the Golden Lion for tea, cake and wine. Capturing the moment, and a fine assortment of headgear, was Bennett the photographer, from St Ninians.

Bridge Clock Tower,
Union Street. (E6)

Baby Carriage

It is possible that the handsome baby carriage in the foreground of the previous photograph was manufactured locally. The Stirling Perambulator Works in Abbey Road, Forthside were founded in 1861 by two brothers, the Messrs Banks, who were bought out by William Clark McEwen in 1881. By 1910 five pram manufacturers were operating in Scotland, McEwens being the longest established. From McEwen's catalogue, trendy Edwardian parents had the choice of yellow pine (with or without hand-painted side panels), walnut, or cane for their offsprings' transport, an example of a cane carriage being seen here. In common with other Stirling firms, McEwens had a substantial overseas market, with infants in Canada, India, South America, South Africa, Australia and New Zealand comfortably cushioned in a McEwen's suspension sprung pram. The company did not limit itself to perambulators, however; it also had a fine line in invalid carriages and in delivery barrows, and the editor of 'Industries of Stirling and District' noted with regret that a shipment of rickshaws for the African market had been destroyed in an earlier fire.

The Stirling Perambulator Company was bought over by Cradle Care in 1987 and as such still operates from Forth Street. Prams have not featured in their catalogue for many years, nor, alas, have rickshaws.

Baby carriage. (F7/8)

Kemp and Nicholson

From Dollar to Dublin, Gartmore to the Gold Coast, the name Kemp and Nicholson was a byword for quality and innovation in the world of agricultural engineering. The firm was founded in 1848 by John Kemp, a joiner and cartwright, in premises in Waughes Pend, Murray Place, opposite the site of the former Baptist Church.

Two partners, Murray and Nicholson, both joiners, joined the firm eventually, Kemp developing an agricultural section. Throughout the 1860s, the firm traded extensively overseas, and Kemp's own design of reaping machine collected prize medals at many international exhibitions. By 1884, expansion was essential, and new premises known as the Scottish Central Works were built at Forth Street. The firm went into liquidation in the early 1930s, an unfortunate victim of the Great Depression.

Kemp & Nicholson,
Forth Street Works. (F7)

Auction Mart

Today's youngsters who slide down the water chutes at the Rainbow Slides Leisure Centre will have no memories of the Livestock Marts cattle market which used to occupy the swimming pool site, nor will they remember the Regal Cinema, seen in the background (left). The Mart extended from the end of Wallace Street (lately Comet car park), right along to the bridge at Seaforth Street. This photograph of the sheep market was taken by the late Mr Andrew Ross from his home in Park Place, and shows the last ram sale held before the Livestock Mart moved out to its present site at Kildean.

The Regal, in Maxwell Place, was one of the ABC Group, and, according to the *Stirling Observer*, its opening ushered in the age of the super-cinema. Stirling supported its cinemas enthusiastically, having the choice by 1936 of the Kinema, The Picture House and the Queen's in addition to the Regal itself. The Allan Park, another super-cinema, opened in 1939, and is still going strong as a cinema and bingo hall. Here the Regal is decorously decked out in bunting to mark the coronation of King George Vl in 1937, but it was the unlikely scene of near riots in the late 1950s when Bill Haley and the Comets erupted onto the screen in 'Rock Around the Clock'.

(above) Livestock Mart.
(G6)
(left) Regal Cinema.
(G6)

Royal Electrical & Mechanical Engineers

Taking the march past on the occasion of the tenth anniversary of the formation of the Royal Electrical and Mechanical Engineers is Provost Hamilton Watters. The ceremony took place at Back o'Hill Camp, now an industrial estate, where military personnel living quarters were situated. Each morning regulars and national servicemen alike had to march from the camp to REME Command workshops at Forthside, closed in the 1960s after National Service ended. Also in the photograph is Lieutenant Colonel R.W. Hearn MBE of the 26 Command Workshop.

REME march past. (E5)

Whinwell Children's Home

All dressed up in their best are children cared for at the Whinwell Children's Home in Upper Bridge Street, founded by Miss Annie Croall. She came to Stirling in 1873, following her father's appointment as first Curator of the Smith Art Gallery and Museum, and dedicated her life to evangelical and philanthropic work. Her first venture was to organise a Young Women's Evangelical Mission, which although concerning itself mainly with its users' spiritual welfare also made sterling efforts to improve their material lot as well, and a four – roomed house in Broad Street was purchased to provide a respectable lodging for destitute woman in 1880. Springfield House in The Craigs was later rented for this same purpose, but it changed in 1887 to a 'Home for Destitute and Neglected Children'. By 1890, larger premises were required, and Whinwell was bought for £950. The first case was discovered by Miss Croall herself, a tiny baby, criminally neglected, and abandoned by its drunken mother who later died. The infant was looked after, and eventually adopted, as were most of the children taken into Whinwell. The Home was maintained by voluntary subscription. Always beset by financial worries, Miss Croall died in 1927, superintending the work of the Home almost to the end of her life. Whinwell Home remained open until 1980, and there can be no doubt that Miss Croall is one of Stirling's unsung heroines; but for her, literally hundreds of children would have endured lives of unmitigated misery.

Children on the step at Whinwell Children's Home. (F6)

Viewfield Street

Two little girls and their father look down from their first floor flat in Viewfield Buildings, Viewfield Street, on to the bustling scene below them, the Jubilee Fountain being the marshalling point for this meeting of the Grand Lodge of Scotland. The suggestion of a fountain to mark Queen Victoria's Golden Jubilee was put forward in 1887 by a Councillor Dowdy, a local hotel-keeper. Barnton Street was chosen to be the site of the fountain, and by November 18th it was installed and ready for the official opening next day. Councillor Dowdy, who had organised the necessary fund-raising, albeit with some difficulty, entertained the workmen to a dinner in his temperance hotel, and he himself switched on the water supply on November 19th, filling a silver jug from which Provost Yellowlees drank the health of the assembled crowd. The all-male guest-list repaired to the Council Chambers in King Street for cake and wine. The fountain's glory did not last long however, as by March 1888 the water supply had dried up, and although today the fountain still stands outside the Sheriff Court, its basins are filled with concrete.

Viewfield Street. (G6)

Barnton Street

This photograph, taken in 1935, shows the staff of Lipton's shop in Barnton Street—a very large staff by today's standards. When war broke out a few years later, most of the young men here were called up and the shop was staffed mainly by women.

In those days customers got personal service and their purchases were tied up in a brown paper parcel with string, ready to carry home. All members of staff had their hands and nails inspected before they went down to the counter and they were expected to wear a clean white coat and apron every day.

Lipton's, Barnton Street.
(G6)

Recruiting Office, South Church

This First World War recruiting office in the South Church, Murray Place (now the Baptist Church) was established in 1914 before conscription was introduced.

The Argyll and Sutherland Highlanders recruited local men but many also went to fight with other regiments. The war brought an influx of soldiers to the town. Local buildings like the Smith Museum were occupied for military use as barracks.

In 1917 King's Park was ploughed up to grow crops. Rationing was also introduced on many items and the 'national loaf', with a lower wheat flour content, became standard.

The war memorial in Stirling testifies to the devastating loss of young men from Stirling during the First World War.

Recruiting Office, South Church, Murray Place. (H6)

Murray Place

During World War 1, the plight of the refugees in war-ravaged Serbia prompted national appeals for help. A local committee was formed, which organised all sorts of fund-raising events – soirees, tea-dances, afternoon concerts, and the inevitable flag-selling. This group of young flag-sellers, photographed in January 1916, were well happed up against the rigours of a Scottish winter, and sheltered from the elements in the Arcade, just in front of the Alhambra Theatre.

Flag sellers outside the Alhambra Theatre. (H6)

The Alhambra Theatre

Originally called the Arcade Theatre, the Alhambra Theatre or Variety House in the old Arcade was a popular venue for Stirling people. Its design was included in the Arcade when it was built in 1881/82. There was much concern at the time over the safety of the structure and a great deal of discussion took place over the strength of the load bearing pillars.

The Theatre hosted a variety of shows from music hall to the Christmas pantomime and also an occasional film. Great Scottish music hall stars such as Will Fyffe appeared there and at times it achieved notoriety as a place of 'low' entertainment.

Its name was changed to the Alhambra Theatre in 1936, but eventually it fell into disuse in the 1950s, and finally closed in the mid 1960s.

The Alhambra Theatre. (H6)

The North Church and the Baptist Church

Both the Baptist Church (left) and the North Church are now demolished. The North Church opened for worship in 1842, to accommodate artisans and business men who had moved, with their families, from the Top of the Town, to new housing in the streets opening up around what is now the town centre. The congregation was relocated in 1969, moving to the Braehead district. The Baptist Church was built in 1854, the design of William Mackison, an architect who, with his uncle, Francis, was responsible for much of the Victorian newbuild in Stirling and in Bridge of Allan. Its distinctive frontage gave it the security of listed building status, which required the purchaser, when clearing the site, to ensure that the frontage was preserved in its entirety. Removal was completed successfully, but while being transported to its new site, it slipped from the lorry, and was shattered beyond repair. The Baptist Congregation moved across the road to what was originally the South Church in 1989.

Baptist Church and North Church, Murray Place. (H6)

Murray Place

Until the mid-nineteenth century, the main route north through the town was by King Street, Baker Street and St Mary's Wynd, to the Old Bridge. For many years, the mart was beside Gowan Hill, and the chaos caused by drovers urging their charges along these narrow streets and the same route in reverse by those en route to the Falkirk Trysts, moved the council to grant permission for the drovers to use Mill Street instead (now Murray Place). At the instigation of William Murray of Polmaise, a new thoroughfare was laid in 1842, and duly named after him. Maxwell Place was called after his wife, Ann Maxwell.

(above) Murray Place, looking North. (H7)
(below) Murray Place, looking South. (H7)

On the right of this postcard view of Murray Place, looking north, is the entrance to the Olympia Pictures Hall. To get to it, patrons had to negotiate the Olympia Steps, which they had been doing since the turn of the century, the Olympia having been entertaining Stirling since then as a cinema, a variety theatre, and a roller skating rink. It went up in flames in 1921, a witness maintaining the blaze surpassed all previous performances.

The ornate building opposite the Olympia, on the corner of King Street, was erected in 1862 as new premises for the expanding Drummond Tract Enterprise, but by 1887, Drummonds had outgrown even this palatial establishment and moved to yet larger premises in Dumbarton Road (now housing Scottish Power). By the time this photograph was taken, the British Linen Bank had moved in, but the carved angels (top left) installed for Peter Drummond remained, the legend, 'Thy Kingdom Come' (chiselled beneath their stoney feet) reflecting the philosophy of their first owner rather more accurately than that of their second.

At the far end of Murray Place is the frontage of the North Church.

This second view of Murray Place looks south, towards Hugh Gavin and Son's drapery shop at the bottom of King Street. The junction of King Street and Port Street

was the terminus for the Stirling/Bridge of Allan Tram, the Railway and Commercial Hotel being conveniently sited at the beginning of Port Street. On the right of the photograph, above the awning, is another branch of the Drummond family – the seed merchants, and Gavin's too was originally Drummond property. Just down from Drummond's is the entrance to the Golden Lion Stables, Crawford's Glass and China Warehouse, and Thomas Lamb's Cycle Depot.

Thomas Lamb's Cycle Shop

Thomas Lamb's was one of at least three similar emporia. His own make was the 'Rock', but he stocked other well-known names of the time; 'Triumph', 'Riley', 'XL', and 'Calcot' all featured in his advertising, which also offered, in 1897, hire facilities to ladies and gentlemen. This reflected the considerable national popularity of cycling, in spite of rough roads and solid wheels. Stirling was the headquarters of the Scottish Central Cycling Association; vociferous representation from such groups persuaded William Ballantine, road surveyor in East Stirling, to purchase Scotland's first steam driven road roller, resulting in an easier ride for the cyclists, well before the demands of the motor car led to further improved road surfaces. In later years, when bitumen surfaces became the norm, the 'tarry boiler' became a familiar sight, like this one in Randolph Road.

Thomas Lamb's cycle shop interior.

Tarry boiler. (L6)

[33]

The Drummond Fire

Drummond's was destroyed in a fire on 23rd August 1949, and neighbouring buildings as far up King Street as the Golden Lion Hotel, suffered severe damage in the blaze. This photograph was taken the following morning by Mr J Gavin who lived in the flat opposite. A keen amateur photographer, he not only made the camera with which he took this photograph, but also the enlarger used. Through the desolate remains of the Drummond building can been see the back of the Golden Lion Hotel.

The Drummond Fire.
(H6)

Port Street

Opposite the foot of King Street, conveniently placed at the terminus of the Bridge of Allan tram, was the Railway and Commercial Hotel in Port Street. For many years, the licensee was Miss Langmuir; on her retiral in May 1904 this photograph was specially commissioned, and presented to her by a group of her regular customers. Note the animal carcass hanging outside the butcher's shop, in just the right place to catch all the dust and flies from the horse tram.

Railway & Commercial Hotel. (H6)

Port Street

What is now Marks & Spencer in Port Street has had a chequered commercial career, firstly as a brewery, then as a woollen mill, and latterly as the premises of William Kinross and Sons, Stirling Carriage Works. Of the firms mentioned in this book, Kinross is the oldest, ousting D & J McEwen by two years. Founded In 1802 by William Croall and William Kinross, it carried on its business in Shore Road until 1865 before moving to grander premises in Port Street. Kinross was another success story of its time, becoming carriage-makers to Queen Victoria, and carrying on a lively export trade. This was not restricted to carriages; a Victorian 'brain-drain' saw several Kinross-trained coachbuilders make their mark overseas. The firm remained in Port Street until the 1960s, when it moved out to St Ninians, closing shortly after.

This photograph of the works was taken in 1923 from a flat opposite, in what is now Littlewoods. The two gentlemen at the door are John Booth and his friend John Rankin. Mr Booth joined the firm in 1921 as a coach body-builder; his hourly rate of pay was 1/7d.

Exterior of Kinross's.
(H6)

King Street

The original Meal Mercate, King Street later became known (perhaps ironically, as it was far from being the wide thoroughfare it is today) as Quality Street, eventually and formally being renamed King Street in 1821 in honour of King George IV. It has seen many changes over the years; shown here are the shops at the top of the street in the later years of the nineteenth century before the arrival of McArees, and the Clydesdale Bank on the corner (now a pub).

Quality Street, formally renamed King Street in 1821. (H6)

Appropriately assembled outside Dowdy's Temperence Hotel at 5 King Street is the Independent Order of the Rechabites, one of many Friendly Society-based organisations formed in the early 1800s to combat the considerable social evils of alcohol. The 'Rechabites' were strongly family orientated with female and junior sections, and were administered by Districts, and 'tents', the banner heading this 1909 procession from the Guardian Eagle Tent in Falkirk. Temperence Hotels, tea rooms, and the like proliferated from the mid 19th century, offering respectable accommodation or refreshment in alcohol free zones well away from the temptation of the demon drink.

Embracing the steepled building at the top of King Street is Spittal Street, to the left, and Baker Street to the right. Now generally referred to as 'The Steeple' it was built in 1816 and known as the Atheneum with shops at ground floor level, a library and reading room above, for the use of the town merchants. The young Peter Drummond, still involved in the family seed business at Coney Park, moved part of the business to the Atheneum in 1831, setting up an 'Agricultural Museum' which from its description was more a showroom of the latest agricultural and horticultural developments than what is regarded as a museum today. The Atheneum was taken over by the Council in 1875, and a statue of William Wallace, placed above the stone canopied entrance, still surveys the passing scene, one of Stirling's best known landmarks.

King Street, Rechabites March. (H6)

On the opposite side of King Street from Dowdy's Temperance establishment is the Golden Lion Hotel. Even the most cursory glance through back copies of Stirling newspapers reveals that, like today, after many public events it was de rigeur for invited guests to be entertained afterwards – cake and wine perhaps, or afternoon tea, and the 'Golden Lion' was a popular venue. In earlier years, it was merely the 'Red Lion', having started as Wingate's Inn, and it was Wingate's which welcomed Robert Burns in 1787. During his sojourn at the hotel, Burns scratched the infamous 'Stirling Lines' on one of its windows. Officialdom was unamused by the anti-Hanovarian sentiments expressed, so much so that Burns returned to the Inn some months later and smashed the incriminating pane. The pieces were carefully preserved by successive astute owners, but finally were destroyed in the blaze of 1949. A handsome statue of the eponymous 'King of the Beasts' was regilded in 1994 and replaced above the hotel after an absence of several years.

The story of Graham and Morton, house furnishers par excellence, is one which mirrors that of many local firms, and epitomises the Victorian ethos of enterprise and innovation. William Graham, a Stirling man, set up an ironmongery shop in Baker Street in 1830, moving to King Street some years later, and appointing his assistant, David Morton, a partner in 1861. Graham & Morton continued to specialise in ironmongery; during the 1870s they employed over 20 nailmakers, and the King Street store stocked everything from kitchen ranges to brass bedsteads. A house furnishing department was opened in Dumbarton Road, in spacious new showrooms in the Wolf Craig building, next to Peter Drummond's Tract Depot. Here Graham & Morton employed display techniques similar to those of today, with suites of rooms furnished and displayed to advantage, the displays changed regularly to tempt window shoppers. Paterson's carpet mill at Burghmuir was bought over to make way for cabinet making and upholstery, and a branch was opened in Falkirk in 1907. From house furnishing, Graham & Morton turned to removals, and it was a logical step from that to house agency. Graham & Morton continued to furnish Stirling homes until the 1980s, when changing consumer patterns decreed its demise.

(above) The Golden Lion Hotel. (H6)
(below) Graham & Morton. (H6)

Baker Street

Originally Baxters Wynd, on account of the many bakers' shops, Baker Street was a main route through Stirling, and at the turn of the century supported, in addition to the more mundane boot and shoe makers (5), licensed grocers (6) and drapers (4), a clogmaker, a venetian blind maker, and a conjurer.

(above) Baker Street. (G6)

(left) Second-hand dealers and pawnbrokers, such as Illingworth's at 82 Baker Street, and neighbouring Hills, were familiar sights as unemployment, poverty, and poor housing conditions eroded standards of living. The contrived cheerfulness of the detergent advertisement contrasts bleakly with the implicit message of the poster beneath it – 'Volunteers wanted immediately, both men and women' – a recruiting drive for ARP Wardens, and a foretaste of World War 2. High on the top right-hand corner of the bill board (rather above eye-level of the average passer-by) is the Lion Rampant, symbol of the 1938 Empire Exhibition held in Bellahouston Park, Glasgow, extending an invitation to visit Marshall's stand at the Palace of Industry. (G6)

(left) J M & M Nimmo's, which many will remember with affection. The buildings beyond and opposite are now demolished.

Lawson's Limited

In 1856, Robert Lawson set up a modest business in Port Street, with the intention of catering for 'the personal and housebound requirements of the Industrial classes.' That he did so with spectacular success is reflected in the firm's need to find larger premises, moving first to Barnton Street and then to Friars Street, before settling at 'The Trades Clothing and Furnishing House' at 32-38 Baker Street, on the corner of Dalgleish Court. By 1894, Lawson's empire had extended to twenty stores, as far apart as Aberdeen and Hawick, Ayr and Arbroath, a branch in Dundee being under the eye of Robert's brother James. The 'Trades Clothing' building housed drapery, clothing, and outfitting, plus workrooms, then in 1899 extensive new premises going right through to Spittal Street were built across the road at number 25 Baker Street for household furnishings. Lawson's survived war and depression, but eventually succumbed to take-over and chain-store competition, closing its doors in June 1993.

Robert Lawson, the firm's founder.

(left) 25 Baker St. (G6)
(above) Sales representatives.
(below) Interior view with customers.
(inset) Interior view – Coronation year 1953.

Stirling Co-operative Society

At one time, the Stirling Co-operative Society had substantial property holdings in the town. Shown here is the grocery in Bow Street, in the Top of the Town. The photograph was taken in 1938 by Walter Gillespie, the then Burgh Architect responsible for clearing the area. Next door to the Co-op is Noterangelo's Ice and Fish Restaurant, a favourite haunt of pupils of the High School of Stirling situated at that time in nearby Spittal Street. Outside the door is Mrs Eva Vettraino, with baby Benedetto in her arms. The business moved to Falkirk shortly afterwards.

Stirling Co-op in Bow Street. (G6)

Broad Street Brewery

The Broad Street Brewery photographed here at the turn of the century was owned by Mr James Duncan and was referred to locally as the 'splash mill.' Mr Duncan was founder of the firm of James Duncan in Drip Road, now known as Duncan's Soft Drinks.

Looming above the brewery is the Tolbooth. A Tolbooth has stood on this site for several centuries, but this building dates from 1703, and was designed by Sir William Bruce, the architect of the Palace of Holyrood House and a former Royal Master of Works. In spite of this impressive professional lineage, he incorporated only 1 prison cell, but perhaps he did not anticipate much trouble from the good burghers of Stirling. Eventually, even the judiciary was moved to comment on the appalling conditions suffered by those incarcerated within its walls, and a new prison was opened in 1847.

Broad Street Brewery. (G5)

Bruce's classical style structure did make some positive impression however, as it is thought to have been the inspiration behind the Alloa master mason, Tobias Bachop's design for the Midsteeple in Dumfries.

Stirling from the Castle

This sweeping view over Stirling, from the Castle, may be dated more readily from what is <u>not</u> there, rather than by what is. Today, the gardens opposite the villas on the right are the home of the Smith Art Gallery and Museum, so its non-appearance places the photograph pre-1873, when the foundation stone was laid. It is probable the photograph was taken in the mid 1860s.

Overlooking the scene is the Church of the Holy Rude whose congregation was so severely split by disagreement over degrees of adherence to the Solemn Covenant, that a solid wall was built in 1656, physically dividing the church into East and West. This unhappy, if not bizarre, state of affairs continued for over three hundred years, and not until 1935 were the two congregations re-united, and the church restored. Snowdon House, centre front, was the home of Dr Doig, revered dominie of the old grammar school, now the Portcullis Hotel.

Sweeping view over Stirling from the Castle.
(G5)

Martyrs' Monument, Church of the Holy Rude

These Edwardian companions contemplate the fate of the Wigtown Martyrs, two women condemned to death by drowning in 1685. The monument was commissioned by William Drummond, a local seed merchant who also landscaped part of the graveyard – a subtle piece of advertising. From their glass walled sanctuary, the marble maidens, victims of seventeenth century justice, look across to the gravestone of an administrator of nineteenth century justice – Alexander Meffen, first Chief Constable of Stirling (on right). A native of Aberdeen, he began work in a mill, before enlisting with the 78th Highlanders, a move which stood him in good stead for his next post, with the Glasgow Police Force. Following service here, he spent five years as 'Chief Detective Officer' at Dunblane, finally moving from that hot-bed of Victorian crime to Stirling. Constabulary duties aside, he was a commissioner for the Forth Salmon Fisheries, and died in 1867.

Holy Rude Graveyard.
(G5)

Walking The Marches

Walking the Marches was an ancient ceremony in which the civic leaders walked, or in some cases rode around the boundaries of a burgh or town every 7 years to mark its limits. In Stirling this duty was carried out by the Provost, the Town Council, the Incorporated Trades and Merchant Guildry.

Walking the Marches

After taking an oath to perform their duties faithfully the company split into 3 groups and on various points on their walk marked the ground with pick axes and spades as a symbol of the rights of the burgh. Farms were visited along the way and the farmer was obliged to provide refreshments. In the evening a dinner was held and toasts were made to the health of the burgh.

Glengarry Lodge

Glengarry Lodge, at 56 Spittal Street, began its existence in the mid seventeenth century as the home of Robert Russell, one time provost of Stirling. It later became an Episcopalian Chapel, serving the community rather differently during the early twentieth century as a lodging house. Often referred to as 'The Darrow Building', it was thought to have been the town house of a Sir James Darrow and built around 1521, but it is more probable that the existing seventeenth century house was built over the site of the earlier one.

Glengarry Lodge. (G6)

Spittal Street

The erstwhile fleshmarket, between Spittal Street and Back Walk, in what is now Academy Street, was the inauspicious site for the High School of Stirling. Designed by H W and J M Hay of Liverpool, the High School opened its doors in 1856; a further wing, from the drawing board of a former pupil J Marjoribanks MacLaren was added in Spittal Street in 1889. Thanks to the generosity of Stirling's Liberal MP Sir Henry Campbell-Bannerman, this incorporated a four storey tower topped by a green-domed revolving observatory, equipped with astronomical instruments, the gift of Lawrence Pullar of Bridge of Allan. By 1962, the school roll stood at over 1100, too many for the existing accommodation, so a site for a new school was identified at Torbrex. On 25th April 1962, the then Rector, Mr J Geddes, led the entire school on 'the long march' from Academy Street to Torbrex. The building was bought by a hotel chain, and opened in 1991 after a £5m conversion.

The Stirling Unit of the Forth Valley Health Board occupies the pillared building on the left. Originally the Commercial Bank, it was built in 1825, but became Stirling's first infirmary fifty years later. The inclusion of a fever ward prompted worries that this was nothing short of an open invitation to every fever related disease imaginable, and raised local temperatures to such an extent that fever victims were henceforth isolated at Bannockburn. A purpose built infirmary arose at Livilands in 1928, a major extension added in 1989.

Spittal Street, looking up towards the Church of the Holy Rude, the Forth Valley Health Board, and the High School observatory on the left. (G6)

Corn Exchange

It would be difficult to recognise Corn Exchange Road as it is today from this photograph. Before the present Municipal Buildings were erected in 1918, Corn Exchange Square had been occupied by a hotel and the exchange itself. The square was one of the business centres of the town and the May Fair and October Fair were held there. These were 'feeing' fairs for hiring farm workers on a six month or year contract.

The Corn Exchange was also one of the few public halls in Stirling, so it was a great venue for dances and civic occasions – a great banquet was held in the hall after the laying of the foundation stone of the Wallace Monument on June 24th 1861.

Corn Exchange. (H6)

Municipal Buildings

The foundation stone for the Municipal Buildings was laid in July 1914, theoretically by King George V, but in practice by a local mason. King George and Queen Mary were spending part of their Scottish visit in the district, staying at Dunblane as the guests of the Stirlings of Keir. Local feelings were running high over the cost of the new building, so their Majesties accepted advice to avoid possible confrontation at the Corn Exchange. They arrived at the County Buildings in Viewfield Place from where the foundation stone was laid by electricity. Work on the site was halted during Word War 1, and the new building opened in 1918.

(left) The welcoming crowd outside the County Buildings.

(below) The stone being eased into position.

(left) The Municipal Buildings.

(left) Corn Exchange Square looking East, the Atheneum at the top of King Street. The buildings on the left were demolished in the 1960s in favour of an extension to the Municipal Buildings.

The Smith Art Gallery & Museum

Like many building of its kind, the Smith Art Gallery and Museum was called after its founder – Thomas Stuart Smith, son of a Renfrewshire merchant, also Thomas.

With his brother, Thomas senior jointly inherited Glassingal House, near Dunblane from their uncle, but falling on hard times, he sold his share to his brother. Eventually, Thomas Stuart Smith inherited Glassingal, and went to live there in 1857. The life of a country gentleman did not appeal however, and he sold up and set off for France. Before leaving, he made financial arrangements for the provision of an institute for the benefit and well-being of the artisans and working classes of the town, and shortly afterwards, he died suddenly in Avignon. Plans went ahead anyway; the foundation stone was laid in 1872; a curator appointed in 1873; and in August 11th 1874 the Museum, with Art Gallery, Library and Reading Rooms, was opened to the public, local shopkeepers taking a half-day by way of celebration. Harvey's 1894 Almanac and Business Directory of Stirling notes that while residents of Stirling, Dunblane and Kinbuck were admitted free, everyone else was charged 2d. The Smith was a great success, but by the 1920s the Library, then the Reading Room, were closed, and in the 1970s, there was a very real danger that due to the building's near dilapidated condition, it would be closed down completely. The 'Friends of the Smith' group was formed to prevent this from happening, and since then they have played a vital role in the upkeep of the Smith, and thereby in the preservation of Stirling's heritage.

Smith Art Gallery and Museum, Dumbarton Road. (G5)

Coronation of King George V

Stirling rose nobly to the occasion of King George V's Coronation in June 22nd 1911. A special 'Stirling Hymn' was composed; shops, public buildings, and offices sported elaborate decorations and Miss Bayne, the Provost's daughter, planted a Coronation Oak in King's Park (her father having been invited to the great event itself). There were treats to the inmates of the Poorhouse, gifts to the poor, and even the little lost souls at the Whinwell Home were showered with unaccustomed luxuries, such as chocolate. Later in the day there was a concert in King's Park plus a bonfire in the evening, and the day finished with a bang, with a Royal salute from the Castle.

Stirling Bowling Club, Dumbarton Road. There's more than one way to celebrate a Coronation – Stirling Bowling Club's Coronation Match and, more importantly, tea. (H5)

Sterlini Commercial School

Setting out for their outing to Edinburgh are students of the Sterlini Commercial School. The School was at 1 Dumbarton Road, better known as the Wolf's Crag building, above Graham & Morton. It took its name from the motto on the Burgh Seal – 'Sterlini Opidum' – and was founded in 1905 by Robert C Forbes, a former employee of the 'Stirling Observer', and who is seated second right in the front row. The first premises were in King Street, and was the first business training college in Stirlingshire. Mr Forbes, an examiner for the training of certificated commercial teachers, held evening classes in Doune and Alloa in the early days of the school, and it soon gained a reputation for excellence in all commercial subjects. Mr Forbes died in March 1960, at the age of 81, and the business closed shortly afterwards.

The photograph was taken in Dumbarton Road by W L Craig on a somewhat dreich 30th June 1916, and the outing was an annual event, World War 1 or not. The charabanc, of which this is a splendid example, was a very popular type of transport. In this one, each row of seats had its own individual door, and the windscreen wiper was operated manually by the driver. Early models exposed their passengers to all elements, but this happy group had a hood to pull up should the weather change.

Judging by the puddles on the roadway, that looked fairly probable.

Sterlini Commercial School. (H6)

D & J MacEwen & Co, Stirling

D & J MacEwen, Grocers and Wine Merchants, was a well-known name in Stirling and beyond for over 150 years. Broad Street of 1804 was a fashionable commercial and residential area of Stirling, and the ideal site for the high quality grocery shop opened by David and James MacEwen, two brothers from a long established Crieff farming family. They purchased the site at the corner of Port Street and Dumbarton Road, currently occupied by Littlewoods, in 1826, and opened shops in Bridge of Allan, Crieff, Dunblane, Fort William, Aberfoyle and, in 1895, Killin. This branch was intended specifically to meet the wants of the sheep farmers and shooting tenants and to cope with tourists and visitors 'principally from England'. D & J MacEwen had a substantial wine and spirit department, which included 'Sterlini', their own special registered blend of whisky. To celebrate their centenary in 1904, the firm held a 'Complimentary Dinner' in the Albert Hall, to which all the local leaders were bidden. One of the Drummonds went, but Campbell-Bannerman and the Marquis of Graham sent their regrets. The less rarified supper dance, held for the employees, continued through the night till four in the morning. The firm continued to serve Stirling until the 1970s.

D & J MacEwen, Grocers and Wine Merchants. (H6)

Stirling Observer

Ebenezer Johnstone arrived in Stirling in the early 1820s, taught for a few years then, tiring of the dominie's role, took over a stationer's shop in Baker Street, and the bookselling and printing side of the same business soon after. The monopoly of Stirling's press at this point was held by the *Stirling Journal and Advertiser*, and Johnstone realised the potential for a rival paper when the Journal's owner, alarmed by Johnstone's outspoken political and religious opinions, regularly quashed reports of his frequent public speeches. The first edition of Johnstone's broadsheet, the *Stirling Observer*, was published on September 15th 1836, and selling at 4d, undercut the Journal by 3d. By using the *Observer* to promote the cause of the Free Church, Johnstone enjoyed the support of Free Church sympathiser, boosting circulation numbers to the extent that larger premises were required, and 20/22 Murray Place was acquired in the mid 1840s. Johnstone still carried on a successful printing business, numbering among his clients local luminaries such as Peter and William Drummond, Hugh Gavin and William Kinross. He retired in 1860, and died four years later. The *Observer* was bought In 1871 by two cousins, George Duncan and John Jamieson who introduced a mid week edition and started newspapers for Bridge of Allan and Callander. Jamieson's nephew John Jamieson Munro took the reins after Jamieson's retirement, and the firm became known as Jamieson and Munro in 1912, the stationery and printing side continuing to trade under that name for many years. The present premises were originally the site of four cottages, cleared in 1907 to make way for the *Observer* offices where the paper is still edited, now a member of the Scottish Universal Newspaper Group.

Observer Office, Craigs. (H7)

James Gray and Company, Seed Merchants

Stirling's importance to the agricultural community is reflected in the success of firms such as Kemp and Nicolson, and of James Gray and Company, Agricultural Merchants. Established in 1865, it soon gained a reputation as a supplier of high quality seed; this photograph shows James Gray and Company's shop in the Upper Craigs, c1930. The company's speciality was in the supply of Timothy seed to users throughout the United Kingdom. The growing of Timothy Grass for seeding purposes was confined to the Carse of Stirling and a small area in the Carse of Gowrie.

The company also established overseas trade bringing to Stirling links with, for example, the West Indies and New Zealand, and attended agricultural fairs and shows abroad, often winning awards for seed quality. In 1954 at the Royal Agricultural Winter Fair in Toronto it was awarded the Quaker Oats Company of Canada's Challenge Trophy for a sample of 'Onward' oats grown by Mr John Gray at Hawkhill Farm, Kincardine-on-Forth. The firm closed in 1984.

James Gray and Company, Upper Craigs. (H7)

1 Pitt Terrace

The handsome house at 1 Pitt Terrace belonged at one time to a member of the Morton family of Graham & Morton fame, and was bought from him by the General Accident Fire and Life Insurance Corporation in 1936. The 'GA's first office in Stirling was at 32 Murray Place, but it moved to 54 Port Street (above the then Elders the Bakers), and from there to Pitt Terrace. The 'GA' occupied the basement and ground floor, the rest of the building being variously occupied by a firm of solicitors, a Chartered Accountant, and the Christian Science Church. The Stirling branch of the Red Cross used the annexe to the right of the building. After the 'GA' settled in, this photograph was commissioned from a local firm, C H Chisholm, and made into a postcard. A copy was given to each member of staff, signed by the manager, J T Robertson. Shortly afterwards, the Council deemed the 'GA' roof sign to be unsafe, so it had to be removed and replaced at ground level. There was a large garden behind the house, and from it one could look down on to the rear playground of the Craigs school. The house was demolished in the early 1950s to make way for a new development, and in its place stand a travel agency and a coffee shop.

1 Pitt Terrace. (J6)

The Craigs School

The Craigs School was one of several built after the Education (Scotland) Act of 1872, which made education compulsory for children from five to thirteen years of age and which placed the responsibility for this on the shoulders of local school boards, rather than on those of town councils. The first headmaster was James Todd, a native of Banffshire, who remained at the school until his death in 1899. During this time, the school burgeoned from a modest institution comprising a staff of Mr Todd, one teacher, and a music master, to one where the 'heidie' presided over a staff of 7 teachers, 6 pupil teachers and a monitor. James Todd died at sea, on board the 'SS Sarmation', and was buried in Montreal. A headstone still stands in the graveyard of the Church of the Holy Rude, 'Erected by Friends and Pupils as a Tribute of Esteem'.

(top) The Craigs School. (H7)
(bottom) Class who left as Primary 1 at the beginning of the war, and returned as Primary 6. (H7)

During World War II, the school was taken over by the Army, and staff and pupils flitted to Allan's School in Spittal Street. The two schools led a peaceful Cox-and-Box existence for the duration of the hostilities and the class photograph shown here was the first class to return to the Craigs at the end of the war, having left as Primary 1 and returning as Primary 6. The school was closed in June 1973, then demolished and the space lay vacant for many years. A multi-storey car park was built on the site and opened eventually in April 1995.

St Ninians Tavern

A view of the old Main Street, St Ninians looking North, featuring the St Ninians Tavern at No 146, with Mrs Black's newsagent and sweet shop across the road.

Main Street, St Ninians, looking North. (N6)

Brucefield Dairy

The pend between the Dairy and the Grosvenor Cafe was known as the Candleworks Close from the days when Messrs. McDiarmid and Sons had their Candleworks in at the back.

The Dairy employed a milk boy, whose daily duties involved a morning and evening visit to a farm at Whins of Milton to collect the milk. This was skimmed at the Dairy, which sold milk, cream and its own buttermilk.

The Brucefield Dairy and the Grosvenor Cafe in the old Main Street in St Ninians.

Bannockburn School Choir

Arranged in all their finery are the children of Bannockburn Public School Choir, winners of the Wallace Shield at the Bannockburn Choral Festival in June 1920.

Organised jointly by Bannockburn Town Band and Cowie Pipe Band, the Festival was started up again in 1920 after a break of six years during World War 1.

Although dancing competitions also featured, it was primarily a music festival, and the Wallace Shield was competed for by local schools, who were required to sing two two-part songs. The test-piece in 1920 was the now forgotten 'The Little River', but it was the Bannockburn school's own choice of 'The Piper o' Dundee' which gave them the edge over their local rivals from St Ninians and from Cowie.

The judge was a Mr Herbert Lane, of Glasgow Atheneum, who professed himself "quite uplifted" by the winners' stirring performance. Local bands were also out in force, instrumental music being provided throughout the afternoon by Bannockburn Town Band, Cowie Colliery Prize Brass Band, and Polmaise and Millhall Pipe Band.

Bannockburn School Choir.

Bannockburn Soup Kitchen

During 1921 the export price of coal fell to less than one quarter of what it had been the previous year, and the mine owners threatened wage cuts to the miners. Lack of support from railway and transport colleagues forced miners back to work, but when a similar situation arose four years later, the mining fraternity stood firm, and with support from the TUC, a General Strike was called from 3rd May 1926.

TUC support was withdrawn only nine days later, and the strike was called off on 12th May and the country returned to work – except the miners. They held out until November, then hunger forced a return to lower wages and longer hours. During the strike period, hardship and privation had been endured by the mining communities, but they pooled resources where possible, to keep their fight. One way of fighting hunger was a soup kitchen, and the group seen here was photographed outside a wash-house in Bentheads, Bannockburn, which, after a coat of whitewash, was used as a soup kitchen during the strike. Donations were collected from shops, and from those not on strike, and soup was prepared and cooked in the wash house. Miners' wives and children arrived with bowls and jugs which were filled and taken home to the family. It was no matter which pit the miners worked in, the local soup kitchen was open to all who lived in the village. One of the Bannockburn rota was Mrs Lamont (middle row, third right), with her son Andrew in front.

Bannockburn Soup Kitchen.

Bannockburn Co-operative Society

1994 was celebrated in England as the 150th anniversary of the Co-operative movement. While the Scottish Co-operative Wholesale Society was not founded until 1868, many smaller co-operative ventures had been in existence for some time; in Ayrshire, for example, the weavers of Fenwick had organised themselves into such a group as early as 1769, for the purchase of oatmeal. Nearer home, a co-operative group was formed in Bannockburn in 1830. By 1900, the Co-op was a considerable commercial force, and an established part of working class life. Even up to the 1950s, the Co-op van was a familiar sight in both urban and rural communities.

The pantile roof identifies this photograph as New Road, Bannockburn with the grocery van which called at, among other places, Plean and Auchenbowie. One side of the van was made entirely of glass, for customers to inspect the goods inside, with extra supplies carried on the roof. The driver was the late Mr Andrew Lamont, seen here with his horse Jimmy, whose monogrammed blanket shows he was from the stable of Bannockburn Co-operative Society. Fish, meat, greengrocery and bakery were all sold around the countryside, each in separate vans. The bake house was off West Murrayfield, which became known as Bakers' Entry.

Co-op grocery van.

Curling on Polmaise Loch

Curling was a favourite pastime in Stirling in days gone by; indeed the oldest known example of a curling stone (dated 1511) is to be found in the Smith Art Gallery and Museum. Here we see a group from Polmaise Curling Club on the loch at Polmaise Castle; Airthrey Loch (in the grounds of Airthrey Castle, now the campus of Stirling University) was another popular site and there were ponds near King's Park. Stirling's earliest club is Borestone and Stirling, instituted in 1750, and admitted to the Royal Caledonian Curling Club in 1840. The Caledonian Curling Club itself did not come into being until 1838, the 'Royal' awarded in 1851 after Queen Victoria had been shown the finer points of the game in the ballroom of Scone Palace. Women had played the game regularly in Stirling, but it was not until 1972 that the Stirling and District Ladies Curling Club was founded.

Curlers on Polmaise
Loch. (N2)

BIBLIOGRAPHY

The Stirling Journal

The Stirling Observer

Stirling Town Council Minutes

Donnachie, I and Hewitt, G. A. Companion to Scottish History. Batsford. 1989.

Groome, F H. Ordnance Gazetteer of Scotland. MacKenzie. N. D.

Harvey, C. Almanac and Business Directory of Stirling 1806-1894. Harvey. 1894.

Industries of Stirling and District. MacKay. 1909.

King, E. Scotland Sober and Free. Glasgow Museums and Art Galleries. 1979.

Lannon, T. The Making of Modern Stirling. Forth Naturalist and Historian. 1983.

Lannon, T. Stirling's Road to Mass Culture. N. D.

Lucas, J. Co-operation in Scotland. 1920.

McCutcheon, R & B. Pictures of the Past. 1984.

McCutcheon, R. Stirling Observer 150 Years On. John Jamieson Munro Trust and Stirling Observer, 1986.

McKean, C. Stirling and the Trossachs. RIAS and Scottish Academic Press, 1985.

Mair, C. Stirling, The Royal Burgh. John Donald Publishers Ltd. 1990.

The Merchants Guide to Stirling, MacKay. N/D.

Simpson, W D. The Church of the Holy Rude, Stirling. 1967.

Thomson, J M and Strachan, C. From Castle Rock to Torbreck 1962.

Grid References

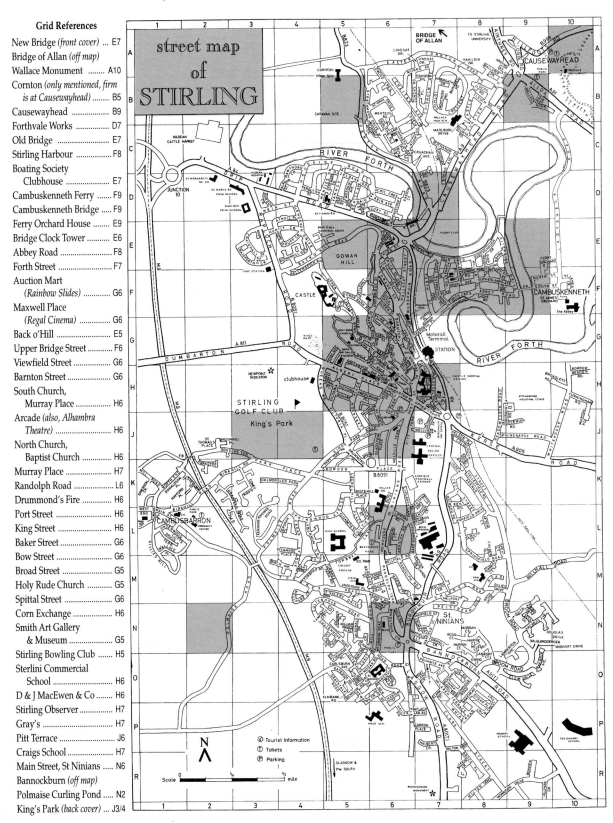